Niiji:

a collection of poetry

Sally Brunk

&

Ron Riekki

Contents

Part *Behzig/Okta*: A Poem by Bamewawagezhikaquay

Le Renne

Le renne est un animal de l'espèce du cerf, on le trouve dans le pays du nord. Cet quadrupède est le principal bétail de les Lapon. Il à la figure d'un cerf, mais est plus grand, et plus ramasse, et les membres sont encore plus délié. La renne donne les Lapons leur lait, et fromage. Les rennes sont plus engraisser dans l'automne et dans l'été. La chair du renne est excellent. La peau du renne—est aussi très utile. La renne est plus égal nécessaire aux Lapons, que la vache est à nous.

Jeanne L. J. Schoolcraft
Decembre vingt-quatre
New York, Mil-huit-cent-quarante-et-un.

published in *The Sound the Stars Make Rushing Through the Sky: The Writings of Jane Johnston Schoolcraft*

The Reindeer

The reindeer is an animal of the deer species, that we find in the north country. This quadruped is the Lapland's main livestock. It has the figure of a deer, but it's larger, and stockier, and its limbs are even more slender. The reindeer of the Lapland give milk and cheese. The reindeer are more fattened in the autumn and in the summer. The meat of reindeer is excellent. The skin of the reindeer—is also very useful. The reindeer is very necessary to the Lapps, even more than the cow is to us.

Jeanne L.J. Schoolcraft.
December twenty-fourth.
New York, One-thousand-eight-hundred-and-forty-one.

[translated from the original French by Ron Riekki]

From my research this piece of writing marks the first time that a northern Native American author writes about a northern indigenous European people (the Saami). Bamewawagezhikaquay is of the reindeer clan and so there's a strong link to the reindeer-focused people of Sápmi. Her writing is a historical moment for transcontinental intertribal connection.

180 years later, this book is a collaborative collection of poetry between an Anishinaabe poet (Sally Brunk) and a poet of Finn and indigenous Saami/Karelian heritage (Ron Riekki). This book is in homage to Bamewawagezhikaquay, to connection, and to friendship.

The narrative continues . . .

Part *Niish/Guokte*: Three Poems by Sally Brunk

Authority Figure

I sit in class watching, observing fellow students trying to outdo
each other,
being "esoteric" using every big word they just learned.
I shake my head, every class the same,
I think, "This is not my version of knowledge,
this is not how one earns respect."

Every day my worlds collide, that 30 minute ride from the rez to campus,
alters my perceptions, flips my world as a shutter closes and
gray area moves in like a fog or thief in the night.
My parents never finished high school,
never went to college, but are two of the most intelligent people I know
respected Elders of the tribe, wise beyond 90% of the people
walking on this campus, than the so called intellectuals,
                    I have to spar with every day.

Walking this fine line between academia and rez life can wear one down,
there is a delicate balance to be maintained,
my family understands the necessity of classes, essays and stories,
but in my mind I think, "This doesn't put food on the table."
....not yet anyway.
Is all this practical?

I laugh and question that every day I cross that invisible line,
that boundary drawn in the sand.
The intellectuals think it's fascinating, interesting to be "Indigenous,"

I'm looked at as a specimen, a rarity, lab rat,
THE authority on Native issues, sovereignty, treaty rights,
Mascots, language, trickster stories, traditions of EVERY tribe in
the country...

Yeah….that's me
I have it all in my back pocket,
but come to the rez, find it for yourself.
Know where it is?
In every pair of Native eyes you see.
Ask them all, every question that fills your book.
You may learn, but will you UNDERSTAND?

The Smithsonian Kidnapped My Great-Great-Grandmother

Long ago when she slept near her home, archaeologists woke her
from her sleep.
They carried her piece by piece, bone by bone to travel in a box,
far from the home that held her spirit, sustained her life.
In the name of science, my Grandmother was poked, prodded,
photographed
with nothing to shield her bones, maintain her dignity.
Catalogued, tagged and numbered, like a specimen or animal in
season,
but not the Grandmother she was.
This museum of science that people run to for knowledge, doesn't know
the first thing about human decency.
Why does it take an act of legislation to hand over all my relations?
Nights that I can't sleep I can hear them,
crying and yelling at their imprisonment,
screaming in rage for their homelands.
All those tribal nations of our ancestors are going to rise up,
storm those shiny doors,
past the exhibits
down winding corridors,
through dusty rooms and confused scientists and
take our Grandmothers and Grandfathers
our relations begging to be brought home.

And you….will not stop us.

Watching the Coming of Rain Woman

I watch her when she silent, and pensive
I see the storm brewing but do nothing
it is as any storm, one can only silently
move out of the way.

No one sees this happening; but we are connected in a way,
Thunderbirds call to both of us. In our dreams, they simply speak.
my niece has the most beautiful cobalt blue eyes, but I must warn you,
the more quiet, pensive she becomes....a storm brews.
Her eyes like the skies overhead, slowly turning from blue to dark gray

With that, her spirit helpers may be warning you, if you can hear
them.
I can, so I can fade to the background, unless I am needed,
I tend to my tasks, and watch her closely. You always take care
of your own.

I have watched this gentle warrior rise up from a tiny quiet child,
she has seen much pain & loss in her young life.
It would cause anyone to crawl into a black cave and never come out,
she sat in the cave for a short time, and came roaring back out.

She has so much power and inherited much of her Grandpa's light,
I believe, she wouldn't let anything or anyone keep her down,
she remembers who she is, where she comes from,
with the ancestors standing firmly behind her.

Her beauty extends beyond her eyes, her smile or creativity,
she spreads love & compassion like her Grandfather did.
It ultimately endears her to people, as they see right to her heart.

It was the same with him, he was loved for his gentleness too.

Yet I have seen the strength of both my parents inside Rain Woman,
times she has felt her weakest, her strength has shown through.
My spirits helpers have already assured me,
my niece is going to, and is, accomplishing beautiful & wondrous things.
I can't wait to see what the future brings to this rising photogra-
pher/writer/artist.

Gimi-wuna-gokwe, I promise to always be there for you.
Me, Grandma & your Mama are your biggest supporters, always,
Know your relations are standing with you, the ancestors behind you.
Keep your tobacco with you, and you can conquer anything.

Part *Niswi/Golbma*: **Poetry by Ron Riekki**

coakh - ká

váib - mu
mu-go
váib - mu

vuoigo
eanan

EANNI,
EANNÁ•AN
váibmu

EANAN

EANNI,
EANNÁ•AN

excerpt
from Nils-Aslak Valkeapää's epic poem *Eanni, Eanná•an*

Ron Riekki's translation from the original Saami language:

meeting

(s)he - art
drum-dance
(s)he - art

bemoans
>> the land

THE EARTH,
>> MY MOTHER

>> heart

LAND

>> THE EARTH,
MY MOTHER

My Sámi Roots

have been cut. Call it an excoriation.
An abrasion. Laceration. My father
has been silent, 70 years, whispering
that we come from reindeer herders.
Sometimes he says we come from rein-
deer. He has told me I am a polar bear,
that my last name has neared extinction;
I was told my whole life it means nothing.
Then I went to Duortnus. I found out
I am a bird, a subarctic mountainside
bird. My father has told me we come
from rain. He says I am always one
degree from snow. Now that he is 70,
he grabs me by the aurora borealis
of my soul and yells that I am Sámi.
I ask him if he can prove it in our
genealogy. He says the indigenous
have been erased, that colonization
happens in the guts. It is deep as
the insides of colons, an ulcerative
colitis. He says that post-colonialism
means the rectum. My Sámi roots
have been tied, scissored, clamped,
clipped. The thick sinew owned now
by Columbus, by Columbine. I ask
him why we are not registered and
deep into community. He tells me
that Sweden did forced sterilizations
to try to make us extinct, that my

grandfather was born one year before
the genocide. I say this in a lecture
to my Performance Methodologies
class. They look at me as if I am
a bird. I am. I feel I should fly
back to Tornio, to Kuusamo, to
Kainuu, where the language is
extinct. Languages die. They
cease to breathe. An infinity
of silence, silence of infinity.
My dad used to sauna 'til he
saw visions. He would saw

them, cut them, slice them,
share them with me. We'd
sit in the steam, the window
showing a lake as quiet as
massacre. Silent, I'd think
of genocide and genealogy.
At least I do now. Then I
probably thought of leaping
into the suicide-water, its
Upper Michigan diaspora.
I'm nervous I'll disappear.
My sister's infertility is
new to us. We process
it. She doesn't cry, not
in front of us. My mom
says she has seen tears
that shear her heart, six
million water droplets
for the 90,000 Sámi
left in the world.

Dad taught math.
He kissed math.
He slept math.
I think now I
understand
why. Sámi
have a word—
jápmigoahtit.
To be on the
brink of death.
Goahtit means
to start to do
something.
Jápmin is
Death. You
can start
death. You
can stop it
as well.
Hoahppu.
Hurry.

i

"You can't do both. There is no such thing as having red and blue together."
Well, the Saami flag has those and green and yellow, so maybe . . . "but no,
things are separate and best understood when separate." I couldn't be white
too. That's just too much. I sat down during a lunch for a job interviewer
and one of the interviewees whispered to the woman next to her, "This guy
isn't the Native American, is he?" I didn't explain that there are indigenous
everywhere, even beyond America, that the U.S. isn't the bruised center of
everything. I kept quiet. It made me think of compulsory sterilization, my
silence. Of genocide, my silence. Of Trump's silence on the shooting at
the mosque. Of subaltern silence. Of the Holy Household of the Prophet
Muhammad (peace be upon them) and the significance of silence. Of my
dead ancestors, their silence even when they speak to me. Of the silence
and peace of the Arctic, with its reindeer silence. Of polar bear silence.
Walrus silence. Beluga whale silence. Ringed seal silence. Critically
endangered silence. The way things lessen slowly, barely noticeable.

I Read that Lapland Looks a Bit Like Palestine

I was born in the Arctic,
in the attic of Finland,

near Sápmi, in Kuusamo,
where the aurora borealis

attacks the senses, where
the sky is porn, where

the snow is an Attica
prison riot, the will

to survive, where
border shifts, roars.

My ancestors are
reindeer herders,

where life is tied
to lichen. We were

put in human zoos
in London. Every

day of my life some-
one asks me how tall

I am. My sister, it's
the same. We're

Tornio tall. My
ancestors survived.

And died. They lived
off the land, meaning

completely off the land,
meaning in the water,

which is the meaning
of 'north' there, not here,

not 'up,' but in the direction
of sea and lake, where

fish kiss hook, where
canoeing is a dance.

The Saami Word for "To Be on the Brink of Death" is *Jápmigoahtit*

It's one word.
Who can speak multiple words when they are dying?

In the tundra,
Death likes to show up in its elegant ballroom silk;

He is always
hungry from someone cold. When I taught in prison,

the student
in the front row had a yellow dragon tattoo across

his forehead,
cheek, and neck. He looked like he'd die soon.

In Saami, the 'Arrow of the Sun God' is *'Njuolla* of *Biejje'*

I wish to be a prophet.
I'd softly violin the world or
at least bust open the mausoleum
of living, the hunched over concept
of living where we are the epitome
of kyphosis, the lungs partially
collapsed and just waiting
for gusts of the divine.

Great

My heart is hermetic.
I am a hermit, someone
who has never met
a her, not even the Father,
lost in my indigenous
desires, my *savage*
wish to save this world,
salvage it from its drowning
tides of slavery. In Canada,
slaves were largely Native
American. We came here

as Native Europeans
of Sápmi—derogatory
term 'Lapland,' with its
strange connotations
of laps, those who sit,
lap dancing, lapping
up water from a lake—
came here to teach
reindeer husbandry
to the Inuit. The soft
fluttering sound

of a Siberian jay
nibbling traded for
the hilarious
white-in-winter

willow ptarmigan,
laughing so far
from the silence
of the extinct auk
or Eskimo curlew
or the extinction
of our language.

Nine Writers of Saami Heritage:

1)   Amoc
2)   Marja-Liisa Olthuis
3)   Pekka Sammallahti
4)   Ánde Somby
5)   Marry Áilonieida Somby
6)   Inghilda Tapio
7)   Johan Turi
8)   Nils-Aslak Valkeapää
9)   Ellen Marie Vars

I

My poetry hasn't revealed my heart. I want to let you inside my fracked guts. I have been a Porter, a door-holder for the military, when (and I've never said this before but) I have Middle Eastern roots, tangled branches of Islam at my core. I was talking with a taxi driver in Iran after I got my DNA results back and he said *Don't tell anyone.* Why? *Because this country is racist as hell, especially against us. I'm serious, don't tell anyone.* My ancestors wore headscarves, hijab. I scream that I am also Saami, Karelian, so there is a looooooong cemetery on my back. I'm crying writing this, but I'm kind of a moron. No one knows me. I am not very important. I don't even own a bookshelf. I have slept on the floor most of my life. I am umber. I am hate-gray. I was not fooled, but I have been a whore-chamberlain. A valley. A blend of coughing and *ugh.* and when I was working in the box office a co-worker took me outside for a smoke break and told me horror stories of when he was in prison that were so filled with split-open bellies that no well could hold all of the choirs of its terror. I am not an expert. Don't read my poetry as non-fiction. Read it as pain. I grew up in the kidneys of the unemployed. I do not have the beauty of having everyone. I am terrified of this life. It makes me feel like the homeless man outside of the frat party, with his beard on fire. In the military, I had to pick up road kill. We did it in the sun, the flies like berries. Ten hour shifts of fur and dried blood. We ate years like that. When I worked in prison, I was attacked, piss and blood in the eyes that the doctor said was nothing to worry about. I put that in as many poems as I can, because I have to put that in as many poems as I can so that

I don't kill myself but instead keep myself alive because the indigenous in me needs survival like a quaking electoral college will lynch and lynch and lynch and lynch and lynch and lynch and lynch until the ghosts of America fill every single second of their hellish, hellish woods.   Bone.   Bone.
Bone.   Bone. Bone. Bond.   Before we die.

I Did My Genealogy

and traced back to find
that I was not Finnish.
I was not what I had adjusted
my body to be. There was
no Finn in my blood,
no window of snow
in my soul, until I discovered
that I was both Swedish
and Saami, both colonizer
and colonized, ripped
in half by history
with my eyes plucked
to one side
and the other, split,
grown into a new *thing*
where I sat in class
and shook my head
at nothingness, lost
in a jar, sightless,
indigenous with nose
measured by those
who accused me
of witchcraft; it was all
laid out, the strangest notes
of your great-great-great-
great-Other, the ones
who died like water,
compost and colonial posts
and colon cancer before

colon cancer was colon
cancer, just a devil
in your sides, and yet
also Swedish, a country
that did its own ethnic
cleansing that no one ever,
ever,
ever
talks about,
except now,
except here,
with my death
in two coffins,
my head
strapped to my back
as I walk
through the bones of my bones

Discovering You're Indigenous

My mother tells me that genocide
and gynecology, in some countries,
are the same word.

on Columbus Day, no less.
No, there's more. Much more.
All your life you've been
empty white. Leafless white,
except without the autumn.
Working-class white which
is like being a used handcuff.
Then you're told that he's
100%. Not one-sixteenth.
Not a flash of myth. He's thick
with Arctic blood. Native
European blood. Saami blood.
A people the Swedish tried
to exterminate. This is Extinction
Studies. We're talking about
being *frozen* in history.
I tell him he needs to register,
to officially reconnect
with the *Saamelaiset*, but he
explains the compulsory
sterilization, how my grand-
father was born one year before
the eugenics program, that
they escaped, the way that ash
from flame has its diaspora
to the sky.

Frozen

When   I was young
to   punish   you
the   teacher
would   make you
stand
in   the   corridor
halfway between
the hallway
and the   exit,
so   that you'd
have   to feel
the winter cold
coming in
every   time   the
            door
was opened.
She   did   not know
that   I   was
Saami,
a people
of   genocide,
almost made extinct
by   the   Swedes,
but we are   Arctic,
survivors
and snowflakes
to us
are   the stars
coming down

to   touch
skin

        diehtu

In Saami, *juo havddi koivvokik*
        means
'dug their grave for you'

Saami is a language
        critically endangered
like the vaquita

or the siola
        or Sumatran orangutan
Language is an animal

It can be buried
        or it can have peace
in its eyes

In Saami, There are a Hundred Words

for *reindeer*,

a hundred words
for *snow*.

In Arabic

there are a hundred words
for *camel*,

a hundred words
for *know*.

My Son Says Santa Can't Have Raised Reindeer

He doesn't have the body
of a reindeer herder,
he says.

There are no callouses
on his hands,
no muscle from the days

crossing rivers.
I tell him his reindeer fly,
but they are not real.

He says he would rather see
real reindeer cross a river
than fake reindeer cross a sky.

After living a life having people tell me my name means nothing

I find out that my last name
in Saami
means ring.

I find out that I am married
to my heritage.
I honeymoon with aurora borealis.

My father is a sauna

My mother is a bear.
My sister is an ice storm.
My brother is a fox.
I am of the Saamelaiset.
I am a sauna and bear and ice storm and fox.
You can see it in my hybrid skin,
the way that my ice shakes its tail.

III

I stood at the edge of the shore on Diego Garcia and watched the Search & Rescue boats, the plane down, the bodies all shrieked.

When I write poems, I forget that I am going more and more into debt every year, that the odds are I will end up pressed to the screams.

I was an EMT.

I was worried that the EMTs were so concerned about being cool that they couldn't be kind.

I hate cool.

America sells cool.

It elects cool.

It wants endings where the solution comes through bullets, cool ballets of bullets.

My girlfriend asks if I want to go to a film and I say *Only if there's no explosions in it.*

I want to return to the Arctic.

I want to go back to the attic of the world.

I grew up in the attic of the U.S.

I have ancestors from the attic of Finland.

The Swedish did forced sterilizations of the Saami for over sixty years.

I've read that there are only 90,000 Saami left.

I come from a people near extinction.

I come from the center of reindeer.

I think in ice.

I once read a poem written by a woman for a contest I was judging where the whole poem was the words *I AM SO ALONE* repeated three hundred times.

I counted.

Looking back, I should have given her first prize.

I should have given her a call.

I should have given her the strength of my gloveless tears.

I should have killed October for her.

How to Find Out You're Indigenous When You're 39-Years-Old

Do your own genealogy; end up in Kainuu or Kuusamo
at a time when no one was there but the Saami,

a group the world seems to have never heard of,
perhaps because of Sweden's attempts

at making the race extinct. I'm sorry;
this is a poem and I got caught up in history,

the explosions of compulsory sterilization,
how my grandfather was born one year

before the date when we ceased to continue
existence. There are more people in Berkeley

than there are Saami in the world. There are more
ants in my front yard than there are Saami

in the world. There are more letters in the poems
in this book you are reading than there are Saami

in the world. Where I grew up is sometimes
omitted from maps. I have Arctic arteries,

igloo blood, snow in my veins, a craving for camp-
fire and reindeer skin. I tell my father he needs

to register as Saami. He tells me that people
of extinction have learned not to register for

anything. I ask him if he can prove he is Saami.
He tells me that the colonizers want proof,

that they do everything they can to eradicate
proof so that all that is left is their history.

I ask him if I am white and he laughs.

I'm Indigenous as Hell

My father told me I was Saami
ever since I was a little headache.
He built a sweat lodge in our house.

I still remember steam in winter,
his naked shaman body crooked
on the top row. I'd go outside,

the snow so high that I'd walk
off the roof into its banks without
falling. We lived in a north

so north that a few more miles
and we'd have been Canada.
I'd listen to the French radio

in my bedroom and pretend
to understand every word.
I stepped off our roof one

summer, shattering my ankles.
In bed, my father told me stories
of the giants in Sweden that

would come to Sápmi to suck
the souls of humans through
an iron pipe. My father would

act like a giant, his feet spread
wide and an invisible pipe in
his hand, and I could almost

feel my soul leaving my body.
When I finally learned French,
I wanted to forget it; I didn't

know how. When I finally
could walk again, I went to
the shore of Lake Superior

and stared at Canadian shore
on the other side, smoke
rising from a chimney,

Halloween. I could barely
make out children in costume.
I blinked and there was no

one there. My mother told me
that Sweden did compulsory
sterilization of the Saami

for almost sixty years, until
1975. She said that there
are less than 100,000 of us

in the world, that I am an
Amur leopard, a black rhino,
a fin whale, a red panda,

that my heart beats Arctic
blood and that my lungs
have breathed aurora

borealis, that when I write
I am refusing to accept
extinction.

Same

Giitu. You want to blow people's minds? Be multiracial.
America operates on the binary system. Kill the grey.
We're reduced to bone, the infantry of fog. That is hell.

Sápmi

The humming of claiming
your ancestry
for the first time.

There is genocide
in my pockets, but I know
now how hard

my ancestors
ran, their Arctic blood
addicted to air.

They insisted
on becoming future
generations, the same

as the river
persisting on turning its *S*
into an *I*, the way we chisel

walls until there is a dark shadow
of door
and then the body explodes through.

The Last Poem I Will Write about the Extinction of My Ancestral Language

This is the very last basement
to sleep.
Coyote sleep.
Have you ever seen me do anything?
The door, the woman.
You didn't like those?
Not even the entropy?
The difference?
The sacred?
I'm not doing the morbid stuff anymore.
I'm an allusion.
Fireflies chant.
Bears wait.

Elegy to the Saami

We are still alive, endangered,
indigenous, in our country,
border-loosened, drinking north,
the bear rituals of love, of life,
an aurora borealis in our will
to survive, the Arctic blood,
our Arctic blood, and we yoik
in our dreams, we yoik through
loneliness, we yoik through sobs,
we yoik through clouds, through
lakes, through loss, and I love
that I am Saami, I am syrup
and oats and ice-shine and hope.

Asse (Saami for 'Skin')

I once peed next to Werner Herzog. So badly I wanted to speak to him. I have a friend, Tom Bissell, who had the luck of having one of his short stories turned into a film by Herzog. I wanted to shout over the urine that I had flash fiction that could be turned into short films. I had sentences he could make into a two-minute youtube dreamscape. He could piss on one of my words and it'd win a New York VisionFest Outstanding Achievement Award. You couldn't hear his urine though. He pissed silently, as if there was species extinction in the room. I wanted to tell him I'm Saami. He didn't even shake. He just left. I could smell grizzly bear.

I went out to the hotel lobby. I was there driving cretins, hack music industry-actors treated as monarchs. I had a post-adolescent punk rocker who I needed to drive home. I went looking for him. He was wearing Halloween makeup, a sort of camou-Frankenstein massacre. I think it was supposed to be art, or just plain panhandling for attention. His band wasn't awful. It was punk, so you can't grade it. It's like grading a tree. You don't give an F to a raccoon. You simply allow it to eat your garbage.

On the drive, I got brave and asked if he knew Werner Herzog.

"Personally?"

"At all."

This offended him. I wasn't sure if he did know who Werner Herzog was, *is*. The celeb-punk seemed like he was a trust fundraiser, someone who wasn't homeless previously, but maybe pseudo-sorrowfully mansionless in his youth. I looked in the rear-view, at him ogling a meter maid. I wondered what it would be like to crave grilled lobster with miso-chile butter and have it delivered to your bed within minutes, and then order seconds.

I'm a driver. I've driven everybody, which means I've been stabbed and choked and sexually harassed and death-threated and marriage-proposed and violently ignored.

"He's brilliant," I said.

"This car isn't," he said.

I looked at the steering wheel; they always make me think of thoracic injuries. I've been upside-down in a taxi. I've sang on ice. I've died and resurrected in a bus. They always need drivers. It keeps me eating. Otherwise I'd be in some psych ward in some soft prison.

I dropped him off. He walked away. I thought of pulling out my phone and filming him. He walked like Charlie Chaplin on Xanax. He stopped. He walked back towards me. I wanted to film him even more now. It hurt me not to pull out my phone. He motioned for me to roll down the window, but I'd already started the process before he did so.

He leaned in, "There are poor people and there are rich people. You are poor because of everything about you."

I wish I could make this up. He pointed at my skin, all of it.

He walked away, the same mix of alprazolam and *The Great Dictator*.

That moment spurred me to seek counseling. It *spurned* me to seek counseling. It *spurted* me. I couldn't afford counseling. Counseling is for the thousandaires of the world. For those neurotic with the hell of poverty, there is no ease. I called and searched and found that Psych Masters students would do cheap guinea-pig counseling. I agreed to a session. It was dangerous and affordable.

The girl who was my counselor looked like she doesn't own a cell phone for spiritual reasons. She'd only do cold yoga, winter Hatha. I could see her doing the splits in the Himalayas. I wanted her Disneyified Thich Nhất Hanh existence.

I told her about the New German urine, the elite-punk, the poverty curse. She asked what I want to be. I told her *to have the ability to survive*. I made rent by the skin of my teeth, by the epidermis of my teeth, the very outer layer where all of the dead cells live. I told her I googled the punk and his parents were diagnostic-invasive whatevers. She dug deep into the knife in my biceps, the history of the hands on my carotid, the way that drunks and the overdosing and the head-injured strike out at the ferryman. For weeks, she pushed me to understand that, for me, the T in PTSD stands for taxi, that I was not an über-mensch, but rather a proletariat choked by American caste system, that *dig* is hidden within *indigenous* as if there is a constant implication of burial. She asked me about the urine, asked me what Werner Herzog's grunt while he pissed meant to me, as if his urine sang how I need to attempt something greater with my life.

She told me to drive and think. I told her it's all I do. I told her that I'm Saami, indigenous north, that there are only 100,000 of us in the world. She told me to write it down. I didn't know how to write. I took a pen one night and stabbed myself in the leg. Or not stabbed, but punctured. A sort of dot tattoo. I told her about it. She told me about cutting, the neuroscience of it, the need for chemical release in the body, the soothing of bleeding, for some. I told her I punctured myself like that three times.

"Like an ellipses."

"What?"

"An ellipses." She made three periods in a row in the space in front of me.

I stared at the air.

"Write the book," she said, "Of your life."

I went home. I began cutting my autobiography into my body. The scars spelled words no one could read but me. Over months, I started to turn into a butcher shop. I'd look in the mirror and see the book of myself. The fibrosis of letters. Lesions of poetry. I quit the counseling. I drove and cut and wrote my history until my entire story was told on my back and arms and legs and lungs and eyes and throat, recited in a totality of scars.

Song of the Suffering of My Liver

for Bruce Smith

My life has been a Brussels, a flowering of my glands,
chambermaid lungs as metallic as porn industry brands.

There are ports where no one goes, like kisses caked in Coke.
I have an Ashland fetish, where my sleep is made of cork.

This Edgar Allan Poe rib cage, this butter-churned brain.
I say, "yes, yes, yes" when I mean to complain. I have massacred

job interviews to the point cops knock on my windows. I have wanted
dark. I have woken up in bathtubs in Boston in houses where I know no

one. My mother is a wintry dork, as quirky as a rabbit. I have
very bad
addictions where I muffle the past in hermaphrodite hops. The
suicide clock

is blasting at the level of oblivion. I scare people when I round corners.
They ask me if I'm Finnish or if I'm Frankenstein, staring at the
Arctic arc of my hearts.

For the People Who are Indigenous

"the rigors of an Arctic sky"
—Bamewawagezhikaquay

I'm tied forever to history.
We're extinct like the footsteps
on the hardwood floor.

For my people, there are a hundred
words for *snow*, for *reindeer*.
In Islam there are a hundred words

for *camel*, for *know*.
My counselor last Thursday told me
that families with genocide

in their roots tend to pass down
the ability for muscled silence;
there are entire cities repressed in soot

and smoke. I'm sick, wishing
for a knife to slice my guts
open, pull out the forced sterilization,

the way that our bear rituals
turned into McDonald's,
shifted our drum circles

into FM radio repetition.
I have a moon in my chest.
It is on fire.

In Kentucky, During the Job Interview, A Woman Pulls Me Aside and Tells Me I'm Too White-Looking to Be Indigenous

The great thing about poverty is that you get to see all of the blood.

There is so much blood.

I've seen bloody Monopoly boards.

Blood on merry-go-rounds.

Bloody lamps.

Blood on pants and shoes and skirts in hair on noses in noses on eyes in eyes on chairs in chairs as chairs for chairs.

Bloody purses and blood-filled wallets.

I return to the prison job EMT job security job and see bloody lamps—I already said that—bloody glasses, bloody penguins, blood-covered bodies, of course, bodies . . .

Blood summers.

The translation of blood.

The attempted translation of blood.

Unfinished Sonnet 2: Wondering If I Am Indigenous Enough to Write about the Indigenous

They say you can write
about Chicago only after you've left. When
you have to struggle to remember the name
of the street, that's when you can write
about the street. My grandfather, before he died,
told me that he hid his past so that I wouldn't
have my tongue cut out. I look in the mirror,
examining my tongue and wonder how long
it will take before I lose it so that I can tell
the world about it. There are so many poems
about clouds because clouds are swallowed
as easily as water. I look in the mirror again.

Rikkaruohoja

Noin noukit rikkaruohoja,
oi äiti, taimitarhastas
ja kohta kaikk' on puhdasta
sun pienoisessa puistossas.

Mut kohta sydän lapseskin
jo versoo rikkaruohoja -
kun sielläi, äiti armahin,
sa saisit yhtä puhdasta!

by Eino Leino (1878-1926)

Weeds (published in *Gloom Cupboard*)

Like picked weeds, there,
oh mother, your nursery of grey hairs
and here is the point: all is purest—
even the sun is a miniature forest.

But soon the heart is skin,
already weeds sprouting—
there! poor mother;
you are just as pure.

translated by Ron Riekki

Part *Niiwin/Njeallje*: Poetry by Sally Brunk

In Celebration Of Women

Linda Hogan writes:
This land is the house we have always lived in.
The women, their bones are holding up the earth.

It is my Mother, sitting by her lamplight,
hiding her pain from her children,
doing the daily routine that she has done for years,
she has fed children, cooked feast meals,
held her Mother's hand as she passed away,
she held her husband's hand and without fear, gave him a last kiss
& "I love you."
This woman who gave me her knowledge, her heart
has taught me to always be proud of being Anishinabe.

Her bones hold up this earth.

It is my Aunties, living and ones who have walked on,
that have brought up families with tradition, language and songs,
it is these Ogitchedaakwe, women warriors that cried tears
as another child entered the sacred circle to dance for the first time,
as another child started the walk on the Red Road.

Their bones hold up this earth.

It is the Dine' woman, the elder in Old Town, on the streets of
Albuquerque,
who sat and talked with me, shared her knowledge

as she sat on her Pendleton blanket, spread with her handmade jewelry.
She gave me a deal on a beautiful turquoise necklace
because she said I looked like her granddaughter,
a compliment in itself.

Her bones hold up this earth.

It is these Elders who share their knowledge,
who are looking to the young ones to offer the semaa & ask the questions,
they will tell the answers.

It is their bones that hold up this earth.

*But it isn't just Native women who hold up this earth on which
we walk.*

It is the women from hospice who tenderly spoke to my Father,
calmed his fears and showed us how to ease his pain and our own,
day or night they came, without hesitation they helped us,
send my Father out in a good way, the proper way.
These women sat at the wake and the funeral, cried tears with the family,
these women shared our heartbreak and grief,
these women sent us cards, letters and called just to "check in."

Their bones hold up this earth

It is the women of the university, of the business world, in the military,
the ones who fight for recognition and respect,
while gaining acceptance these women give their fellow sisters
advice and support.
Together there is hope and fulfillment and strength in numbers.

Their bones hold up this earth.

It is my fellow sisters of color,
these women keep the bond of family and community
strive for a better world and better environment to bring up our children,
these women teach color is not an issue, color does not define a person
color is not a ruler on which one should be measured.
These women possess such strong fiery spirits.

Their bones hold up this earth, too.

It is every woman who puts pen to paper,
who writes down our stories and helps people to understand,
women who tell the stories weaved down through generations.
It is every woman who stands behind a cause,
who stands against injustice or discrimination.
It is every woman who chooses the road to education,
it is every woman who decides to bring children into this world,
it is every woman who decides to adopt & foster children.

I am thankful to all of my sisters who
day after day, month after month, year after year
continue to hold up this earth,
Who sacrifice their bones, their strength, for the many.

On this day, be proud of yourself. I say simply:

Chii-megwetch, Ogitchidaakwe (Warrior Women).

A Poem Before Breakfast

He was a simple, quiet man, a meat-and-potatoes kind of man.
He never complained about anything and he worked hard,
sick or not, he rarely missed a day.
He loved all sports and it was his release, his relaxation,
he may not have went to church but communed in his own way,
he was thankful every day for what was given to him.
He said prayers quietly for his wife, family and many friends.
He was loved by people, simply because he looked you in the eye,
he was honest when talking; he told it to you straight.
When his journey home started, we weren't ready
but we steeled ourselves for the inevitable...as he taught us.
He changed, became softer, quieter he said, "I love you," more.
He hugged everyone a little tighter, and was happy to simply sit
and hold your hand.
At the end, he was surrounded by all of his loved ones and I knew
he was happy
I knew he was just staying here for us.
I knew he was tired and wanted to leave.
So I did what I had to do and told him, "Let go, Daddy."
And he did.
There will always be a space where he should be, but we know
he is in a better place now.
Where he is, he has no pain, no tiredness, or indecision.
He is simply happy, and at peace.

Abiinoojiins

In the creation of new life
There is new beginnings, new hope
The start of a new chapter of intertwined lives
A child brings laughter and smiles
My hope for you is that your child is blessed

In this small prayer, small poem
An offering is made, friendship given and held
Wishes and hopes for a special family

This child will be loved, and cherished
Beautiful memories and dreams will be realized
With each new step this child makes
With each new lesson learned
Dreams will be realized, each and every day

For you as new parents, I give strength
For all those smiling moments, and trying times
When a child may hurt, may get sick…stay strong
May you gain strength each and every time
A new step is learned, new word is spoken

A child stays a child but a short time
But they never forget where they came from
They never forget the love of their parents
They always realize and run to love of family

May you remember each and every moment
May you laugh each and every day
With this new little one

In Ojibwa "abiinoojiins" means small child
They are most treasured because
They are the hope of a nation
Born to lead and take care of their elders someday
They are given lessons and everything needed
To prepare them for this world
They are protected and loved from birth

May every moment with your abiinoojiins be as beautiful.

Adrienne & Mom

Mom wraps her arms around Adrienne, she is fussy & tired
She is fighting sleep to the hardest extent
I watch Mom's patience, slowly covering this abininoojins
Like a blanket, comes patience and love....sweetness
She is humming one of those early Anishinabe songs that
I remember from my youth
She put me to sleep with that song too
Years later, it still works.
Those weathered, beautiful, scarred hands;
That she believes are so ugly: are long, tapered, deep brown and
gorgeous.
When she argues, I tell her they show, she is a survivor.

She smiles at me, and I realize Adrienne is deep in sleep
Mom also rubbed her little head, no baby can stay awake after that.
I also realize, Mom is also stuck in the rocking chair
Together, we silently giggle at her predicament
So we talk. As we always do.

Akeequa "Earth Woman" — April 30, 2014

You left without saying goodbye; you left sudden, in a rush and
hit that trail for home, smiling because you knew that soon you would
see Daddy, and other relations waiting at the end of the trail
with a feast for you, and open arms.

You heard those traveling songs, listened, and started your journey home.
We had four days to relive your life with you
through memories, stories, laughter and tears.
Singers from three different tribes and drums sang their hearts out for you.
They kept singing as they cried, even as they danced.

Your cousins numbered many on the drum,
men and women alike, and all hurt as much as we did.
There are many ways I can describe you, sister.
But my favorite word to describe you was: FEARLESS

I watched you, when I was a precocious 10 yr old and you, all of 19;
I was in awe, that you took no attitude from anyone.
Yet, not quite surprised at the same time.

Your fearlessness came from strong warrior blood, borne of many
generations,
from Be-Mashi-Kwe and Osac, beautiful Ogitichidaakwe
From early on in our family.
You were giving, loving, thoughtful and simply honest.
You fed and clothed everyone, took in relatives and friends alike,
even though you only had a one-bedroom apartment.

You were one of the most generous people I know,
always telling me, "You never know if the one you help, might be an
Angel."
Wednesday you reach home.

I know Daddy and all the ancestors are feasting and drumming for you
already.
Sister, please know how much we, your siblings love you,
but know that Momma is now missing part of her heart.

With heavy hearts, but smiles for you, we will enjoy this feast with you,
because now, your long walk is over.
Rest now, sister. We are so glad you have no more pain.

Ba ma pii, Akeequa...

Al

When I was a child, *I thought you were Superman,*
the strongest most handsome man I ever knew,
you would throw me into the air
and smile as I giggled uncontrollably.
I loved watching you play softball,
beamed proudly when you hit a homerun,
I would scream to the other kids as we chased the ball,
"That's my Daddy!" *You were always a superstar to me.*
Happiness was riding in the car with you in comfortable silence,
the sky was always bluer and the trees greener, the air fresher….
You brought clarity & security to my adolescence
with your calming presence.
I have watched you be the foundation in which eight children
have jumped off into adulthood;
the man who would rise in the dark hours of the morning
to work eight, ten, twelve hours, never turning down overtime,
because that meant more money for food, clothes….shoes.
Through all my trips in & out of college
you never showed disappointment, but gently gave your
unconditional support and nudged me when I was ready.
I could never say thank you enough for your guidance, strength
and love.
You are and always will be the most important man in my life.
The clay of my existence has been formed by your strong hands.
You and Mom are my pillars of strength.
Chii-megwetch my Father for helping me to spread my wings….
And learn to fly.

Albert Jr.

My oldest brother is a fighter.
See, Al Jr. has to be, he's learned this trait over the last year
since he's been diagnosed with cancer.
But, that is not the only reason I respect and love him.
It is because he has faced this fight with dignity and grace,
with a courage that many could not have imagined
or even accomplished on their own.

With his wife Annie, they have brought up three boys
to be as strong and hard working as they are.
Through his courage, and his struggle these past few months
I have seen true love expressed in so many small, yet important ways.

My sister Nancy calls to check on the two of them and cooks
occasionally,
Mom makes him fry bread and biscuits.
Sister Brenda has drove him to his treatments, yet Annie is his
constant.
She has experienced every single minute with him, has never left
his side.
This is unconditional love too.

Yet my brother is more than this cancer, is more than this fight.
He is someone who loves sports, has played softball for many years.
He is a carpenter, has worked on many homes, including our own.
He loves to fish, and would fish every day if he could.
He is a good brother, great father and better son,
Momma is proud of him and I see it in her eyes every time he
comes to visit.

This fight is not over, and he isn't walking this road alone,
this family is with him no matter how long it takes.
Yet so is his sage, smudge bowl, sweetgrass, tobacco and eagle
feather.
These will sustain him, will give him strength when he needs it.

This fight is one of many this family will face: Together.

Alice Mary

She has four children and
works hard every day to provide for them
she loves being a Mom, and is great at her job.
She is a proud Anishinabekwe,
immersed in our traditions, and
teaching her children our culture and language.
We are overjoyed to be close to her and her children,
our time with her little family is so precious.

She is one of the greatest mothers we know,
who loves unconditionally and fiercely.
She gives everything to the ones she loves,
we're so very proud of the home she has created.

We have watched her grow as a little girl
into a young woman who began dancing
Grandma was so proud when she won Miss Keweenaw Bay.
We have watched her every step into womanhood,
loved her as each child entered our family,
as they received their Ojibwa names, as they began to dance.

She has been there during the important steps in our lives,
always supporting, or putting down tobacco when we need it.
Like her beautiful children, she treats her Grandma as a prized
possession,
she is gentle with her, always listening and grateful to see her
when she can.

Each of her children has their own tastes and personalities,
she has everything to do with that, letting them be themselves.
She is behind them, guiding them when necessary, always supportive.
We love watching her children grow and develop, nourishing their
interests.

She is strong, even when she doesn't believe she is,
she is unwavering, when it comes to belief in her children,
she is courageous, when it comes to protecting her family.

She is a beautiful soul that we will always believe in and support.
We are so very proud of the Anishinabekwe she has become.

All My Relations

All my relations offer tobacco in the sunrise ceremony,
offer prayers for a good day of dancing and singing, of laughter
and good travel,
all my relations setting up chairs and blankets, babies in strollers
and playpens,
standing and sitting together, laughing, braiding hair, telling stories...
Each helping with regalia, piece by piece...

This process a ritual in itself.

All my relations smudging sage and burning sweetgrass,
humbling themselves praying for strength in mind, body and spirit,
for the sacrifice they will make for relations in homes, hospitals
and prisons.
In their dancing and singing each step and each song a prayer.
All my relations gather in the east door for Grand Entry,
jingle dress, fancy, traditional, grass all dancers one rhythm, one
movement,
becoming part of the drum, flag bearers with their heads held high
take the first steps,
all my relations rising from their chairs swelling with pride,
Watching the dancers aware of the Native blood coursing through
their own veins.
All my relations eat a feast meal together: fresh fruit and berries,
venison and wild rice.

This too, a ritual.

All my relations, pool gas money, travel many miles, take time off

from work,
Sleep on floors, sleep on Mother Earth, arrive home with empty
pockets and full smiles,

Just to feel alive.

Annie Mae

Lately thoughts of Annie Mae Aquash fill my head and I wonder,
how long she lay in the cold hard snow before being discovered
by the mixed-breed,
before the FBI came and cut off her hands.

What sounds did your spirit hear Annie Mae?
What animal sounds? What storm surrounded you?
Even Mother Earth cried crystal tears,
the snow freezing to the red blanket in which you were wrapped.

Killed for being a modern day warrior a fighter of injustice,
A woman who protected the future generations,
a woman who valued her elders,
killed because she was seen as knowing too much,
killed because she was a danger to the authority.

Did you feel fear Annie Mae,
as the cold gun was pressed
to the back of your head?
Did you fear the inevitable bullet or
were you fearless in those last seconds?
Was your last thought of
your children and the family
who would be denied the right to
mourn you in the proper way?

I was but a child when you were murdered
        I was told the stories, your legend
I did not read of you until I was an adult

I felt the mystery surrounding your name.
Today, I read of the men charged with your murder,
I wonder as I clutch the newspaper
        with hot tears sliding down my face,
if your spirit has found its peace from that
long ago patch of cold hard snow.

I wonder, has your spirit found its way home?

Anniversary (For Papa)

It will be nine years soon, to say it doesn't hurt is a lie.
I think of him every single day.
I watch my Mother, the gulf she doesn't cross on the bed that
was Dad's side.
The conversations she misses with him the special kisses just for her.
To think of those moments hurts most.

Days that she really wants him with her, she wears his wedding
ring on a gold chain.
She talks to him every day she prays to him on difficult days.
In some way he always answers her.
What to say about the bond of love?

He always comes to me when I need him, he leaves one of my
lights on as a sign.
I merely smile because I am positive he visits, but he is truly
content where he is.
Yet I know he will always watch over us.
This one thought keeps me sane, keeps me centered.

So, on the anniversary of my Father's death I will be happy for him,
the family, knowing we have our own guardian.
I know that he is playing all the sports that he loved.
I dreamed he was playing basketball with all of his old friends,
As long as I believe he is smiling I can smile too.
I will sing your song the rest of my days, nii papa.

Another Breath

My Father never complained about the pain, not once.
Even through the very painful last weeks, he never gave in,
I watched his face, I knew how much the pain affected him,
but it was almost as if he stayed strong for us, the family.
So I smiled as I gave him Morphine shots for pain,
I was gentle as I gave him shots of Heparin for blood clots.
I knew even the whisper of the cool sheet on his skin hurt.

So I stayed.

Through the endless days and long nights,
we all took turns or just kept each other awake,
as we watched his breathing,
and prayed...he would take another breath.

At Sand Point

On a warm summer day, while my sisters were cooling off near
Lake Superior, I wandered farther than I should.
At ten years old, I was caught unaware, playing in the water,
throwing rocks,
going deeper, simply unaware of the depth.
It happened quickly, my foot slipped and my head went under.
Far away, I could still hear my sister's radio,
Brenda was sleeping, Nancy reading a magazine.

I swallowed water.

As any child would do, I panicked.
I flapped my arms, kicked my legs ...but knew I had let myself get
in too deep.

Then I felt a push in the back, sending me towards shore. To-
wards safety.

I whipped around, saw a glimpse of unruly hair...and then nothing.

I found myself on the beach, coughing up lake water. Rushing to
the arms of my sisters.

For days, even weeks I thought about it. Was pensive.
Walked the trails behind our house alone and never told a soul
what I saw.

It never came to light again until my Auntie Joyce's funeral,
where I saw a photo of my Mother, Aunties, and Uncle Billy

(Sonny) as children.
That was the boy that helped me.
My Uncle Sonny who walked on before I was born,
Sonny who drowned trying to save his best friend from the same fate.
Did he save me?

I told this to my sister Sharon, who said,
"Write, and be thankful for guardian spirits." My sister was a wise
woman.

They say Sand Point holds many secrets.
Tomorrow I shall put down semaa, and simply be thankful for my
family and its guardian spirits.

Auntie Bood

Your name was Elizabeth, sister to my Father, Albert,
mother to ten beautiful children, two little girls lost as babies.
You always kept them close in your heart.
My Auntie who I will always miss, grey/blue eyes that sparkled,
grey/black hair pulled into a bun, bright smile and strong laugh for anyone.
You could trap, hunt and fish, my image of strong, sturdy independent.
I often find myself asking, "What would Auntie Bood do?"

Childhood memories of being held by you in your favorite chair by
the woodstove,
your clothes smelling of smoke and cedar, telling me stories until I
gave into sleep.
I pull these memories out, in times of weakness, I carry them
close to my heart.
Grandmother Brunk's daughter, who carried her legacy,
she proudly carried on traditions, taught the children well, com-
forted and supported brothers.

The family is now carrying the legacy for you.

I pray you see this, I pray you know, your memory is honored.
On this day I offer tobacco for you, chii-megwetch for letting me
learn from you.
You came through storms of wind, rain and snow, laughing,
always laughing
All the elements rolled off your strong back,
like the fall leaves I brushed off your spirit house the last time I
went to visit.

Your name was Elizabeth,
we honor your legacy proudly.

Auntie Joyce

I keep you in my thoughts Auntie Joyce, as my day begins,
I offer tobacco for you and the rest of the family,
I have now begun to do those habits that were so lax for such a
long time.
You have taught me to remember those small, yet important steps
in one's day.
I've searched the skies for an answer of why you had to leave,
I look above and see migizi circling and find my peace there.

I keep you in my thoughts Auntie Joyce as I wake Mother for
another day,
you came to me in my dreams, and told me, "Take care of your Mom."
I promised you that all of us, as her children, would.
So as I help her with her daily activities, and as we go about our day,
there is your voice, your smile, your laugh.

As I watched the family this past weekend, as they sang the
traveling songs for you,
I saw how you influenced each one, Auntie Joyce, how you taught
them to be so strong.
Your sisters, to your sons & daughters, grandchildren and nieces
& nephews,
each of them was strong for you, was influenced by you, and
smiled when they wanted to cry.
Your family holds many of your characteristics, your smile, eyes,
laugh, or strong, fiery spirit.
I hope you know we all carry you with us, no matter where we
are, a part of you is always there.

It physically hurts knowing you are no longer in Lac du Flambeau,
yet another part of me feels lighter, better knowing that where you are:
there is no pain, no dialysis, no trips to the hospitals or pills and insulin to
take.
You are healthy & happy and have no worries where you are now.
We are the ones who must find our peace wherever possible and
stay strong as you taught us.

So for you, I will start those connections with the Creator that
have been so sorely lacking,
sweat lodges and teachings, singing with the drum, times that
made me so strong.
I need such connections in times like this, and I can hear your
voice from our morning together,
only two awake, talking as we never had the chance to before.
You, telling me, I need to get back to my place of peace, I need to
find it once again.
I promised you, I would.

Chii-megwetch Auntie Joyce:
for all that you have given me, shown me, shared with me and
taught me.
I will speak of you the rest of my days, and I will never forget
what you have meant to me.

Auntie Joyce II

At times it sneaks up on me,
with casualness, with cunning….before I know it,
the grief is on, choking me and pulling sobs out of my chest.
Most days I can fight it, keep it under control,
because that is what we must do, continue on with the knowledge
that one day, we will see you again, hug you again and laugh with
you again.
Because I still have those days when it hurts like the moment I
first heard,
that call from Karen when our world changed, turned upside down.
The scream that came from Mom is one I will never forget, pure
pain, utter agony,
wishing that what I had to tell her wasn't true.
Every day I pray that where you are, you are alright, whole and laughing,
happy that you are no longer in pain or surrounded by medications.
This, I wish for all the time.

All the time.

Auntie Joyce III

This first weekend in August marks a year that Auntie Joyce has
passed,
I'm told to be happy for her, to celebrate her life, To not cry.
Its not so easy, to accomplish.
But I will be strong for Auntie and my Mother,
that is what Anishinabekwe do.
But I will never forget her smile,
I will never forget her laugh,
I will never forget the love she carries for her children,
her grandchildren or her nephews and nieces.
She had such a strong fiery spirit, just like my Mother.

It is now November, and I am finishing this months later,
because sometimes I have to step back,
sometimes it is difficult to do those necessary
steps that complete us and make us whole.

There was a time after Auntie Joyce walked on,
that nothing seemed right, I couldn't taste anything,
didn't feel like sleeping, I had no want of music or reading,
I couldn't write a single word.

She came to me in my dreams, where our worlds connect for just
  that short time every night before dawn comes.

All she had to do was shake her head and she said one word:
Write.
Like my Father before her, she knew that writing was what would
save me,

my self-preservation kicked in and I did as I was told.

As I typed, wrote in my journal and opened myself
up to the world again, I could see the beauty in everything,
I reconnected with old friends, made new ones,
I could listen to music, close my eyes….and smile.

Auntie Joyce saved me.

So I speak with her, every day.
As I speak to my Father, and other relations that have passed.
I know behind that filament that separates our worlds, she can
hear me.
Chii-megwetch, Auntie.

Auntie Moon

Beading
Auntie Moon beads
Lines of her face lead to a story
Experience and avenue of life
A busy highway with no end
A face dark and beautiful
So like my Mother's
Deep brown eyes of knowledge
Have seen a tapestry of
Tragedy and happiness
Hands that do intricate beadwork
Have nurtured babies, held loved ones
Fought racist people
Small arthritic hands
Have threaded together generations
Memories and a history of ancestors
These colored beads become a legacy
A story to be retold, never forgotten
Auntie Moon beads

Becoming

The spirits talk to me of what to speak of, what to tell
the ancestors of old are there, you just have to
close your eyes, concentrate….and listen.
It is how I make my way
in this world and how I survive.
This is my way of becoming, evolving into the woman,
the Creator is asking of me.
I can only hear and try to answer in this place.
There is no time, there is only existence,
There are no boundaries, no color lines,
It is as one circle.
As the Creator says it should be.

Bede-dway-way-gezhi-gokwe & Nii-gwan-nii-gabo

As I wake for another day, my first thoughts naturally fall to Mom,
I pray that her night was pain free, and her dreams were pure & good.
During her sleep and at night, I become most protective.
    It is when darkness falls, the ancient ones have said; the
spirits roam.
    Are you with us, nii Papa?
    I feel him there, day or night...

It does not bother us, to know he roams & protects our home,
the home he worked so hard to improve before the cancer took him.
    His voice still echoes here.
Some nights, I still hear him calling me through the monitor....

    I smile, close my eyes & say my prayer of thanksgiving for
this day.
Momma is awake; 76 years old, full blood Anishinabekwe,
    born and raised in Lac du Flambeau, Wisconsin,
to Alice and John Kenosha.
She never had the chance to meet her father, who passed away
from pneumonia
    when my Grandmother Alice was pregnant with her.
    His simple words to Grandmother Pine, "Take care of our
little girl."
Momma smiles at me, and everyday I am renewed by her
strength & spirit
    I thank the Creator for her smile every sunrise.
Our morning floats along, we sit at the kitchen table. She talks, I listen.
    Our coffee is therapeutic. Her words flow like the warm

amber liquid.

I close my eyes, simply listening to the rich lyrical tone of nii Mama's voice.

Through her, our ancestors & relations who have walked on are alive once again,

they dance, and within her words, I hear that distant drum we should all listen to.

She has a beautiful voice and when younger, often sang with her sisters.

So whenever we do hear her singing and playing her guitar, we simply treasure it.

At crucial moments during our day, she holds my hand.

Such as, while making a point during a story, or needing my help walking.

I wonder, as we match steps & rhythm, who needs who, more.

Sometimes, I realize...*I, am hanging on too tightly.*

My Grandmothers whisper, "Sally, don't ever forget what she is teaching you."

There is no one in this world that knows me as she does.

She knows my heart, my intent in writing for truth.

For her, and the continuing generations I will stay on my path,

I will be the family storyteller, our nii Papa said I would be,

I'll tell the stories that need to be told....

Chii-megwetch, Bede-dway-way-ghezhi-gokwe & Nii-gwan-nii-gabo,

for continuing to teach me the lessons I need for this life.

Boundaries II

Sometimes, when I wake in the morning,
my touch lamp above my television is turned on.
The big deal? I never turned it on.
I believe it's my Father, showing he's watching over me.
He knows since his death, I have had trouble with
the dark, with dealing with shadow people who
inhabit my room, trying to take pieces of me, of my mind.
So I fight them. I have learned to sleep with a light on,
or the television on, to deal with them.
The only one I have ever asked for help with this is,
my Father. Somehow, he still watches.
That calms me, keeps me sane. Protects me.
Yes, I do believe there is a connection to the spirit world,
one that everyone should remember,
because I know they don't forget us.

Sometimes, when I wake in the morning,
my touch lamp above my television is turned on.
The big deal? I never turned it on.
I believe its my Father, showing he's watching over me.
He knows since his death, I have had trouble with
the dark, with dealing with shadow people who
inhabit my room, trying to take pieces of me, of my mind.
So I fight them. I have learned to sleep with a light on,
or the television on, to deal with them.
The only one I have ever asked for help with this is,
my Father. Somehow, he still watches.
That calms me, keeps me sane. Protects me.
Yes, I do believe there is a connection to the spirit world,
one that everyone should remember,
because I know they don't forget us.

Boundaries

My Father roams my bedroom when I am gone,
he lingers, touches my books and cds, my abalone shell I use for
smudging.
My Mother hears him walking and touching, and sitting in the
middle of my room.
She is not afraid, not surprised because he visits frequently.
My Father who has passed on to the spirit world, still watches our
family, still watches me.
He talks to me, to my Mother and says, "You will be okay, hold
onto each other, to the family."
I know this, am reassured in my dreams by his strong voice.
He whispers to Donna, my four year old niece and says,
"Give your Mom this hug from me. She needs it."
To Donna this is not a shock, it is a natural progression,
this thin line between the living and spirit worlds.
Children do not know how to question, to know there is a differ-
ence, a boundary.
Her mind is open and receptive to my Father and
she was always one of his favorite grandchildren.
He comes to her because she merely sees his death as another
form and that is all.
Children do not know this boundary, this wall we have built
between us and the spirits.
They only see the relations that have come to watch them grow and,
mature through the changing seasons, the many moons that pass.
They only see the smiles just for them.
Today, my one-year-old nephew Samuel Albert (named after my
Father), out of nowhere,
looked toward the ceiling and said, "Grandpa."

He then waved and gave the most innocent smile, then said,
"Where did he go?"
We have no doubt he saw my Father, who seems to watch over
his namesake with extra care.
We smiled and yes, had a good cry, but it also warmed our hearts
at the same time.
Boundaries are nothing for children.
It is only when we grow older that we distance ourselves.
Don't ever forget the spirits.

Celebrating Elizabeth In July

She is woman of quiet conviction, of a strong and open heart.
The beat of her heart is the rhythm by which we live,
and by which we sleep by, this has been, since the day we were born,
It is our connection to her, our invisible bond.

She is a woman of solid determination,
she has been the foundation for eight children,
and countless grandchildren and great grandchildren.
Through her eyes we have been shown the world.
She is our teacher.

Through her, we learn our language.
Through her, we learn our culture.
Through her we are transformed into our own form of being.

She has never turned away a child or a grandchild,
but always welcomed them home,
there is no shame in coming home to family.

We have all received our love of learning from her,
to never stop learning, that is what she gave us,
she is constantly teaching us, each and every day,
how we can better ourselves,
how we can better each other,
to give love and receive.

Together we are stronger because of her presence,
together we are given knowledge to last our lifetimes,
together we shall share her wisdom with the following generations,
she has given so much, and we are thankful for her.

Chii-megwetch Mother for giving me this life.

Daddy

The walk from the house to the field is like its own ritual,
most of the time I am alone, sometimes Brenda is with me,
my feet are in the black Nike baseball shoes you bought me,
we both got a pair remember?
When my feet hit the sand and cross the white lines of the field,
you are with me, I see your face.
In the infield, in my routine of warming up and stretching,
my mannerisms on the field,
there is your voice, your face.
As I walk to the batter's box, I hear the men in the bleachers,
"That's one of Al's kids." And the response,
"If she's one of Al's, she must be good."
As if this is a given.
I still hear your voice saying, "Never swing at the first pitch,"
instilled in me when I could barely swing a bat or lift it.
My glove once held your hand,
sometimes that is what keeps me centered.
You are with me on the field,
you are with me as the game ends,
as I critique my own playing,
as I walk to the house we once shared.
There is your face.

Drums

A warm balmy night, unusual for a UP summer,
My twelve year old legs run out the back door,
down the freshly mowed lawn,
long black hair streaming behind me.
I smell deep green grass, I run towards the fields, behind my
family's house.
I have lived my whole live here.
The drums are sounding, pounding out the heartbeat of Mother Earth
In rhythm with my own heartbeat.
I dance, I twirl, I step, I hear the incessant beat,
even with the mile of woods between us.
I sing along to myself, throw my tobacco to the four directions.
This is what Grandmother tells me,
This is what she sings to me,
This is what she breathes into me.

Essence

As I sit at the kitchen table
I watch my Mother cooking
Memories come back of past stories and moments
She has told me about our family and my Father
About my Grandparents and Great-Grandparents
An invisible cord that is never broken or separated
By the generations
History I am trying to recapture
To embrace
To relive
Through her voice
I become all encompassing when I am around her
As I try to embrace and soak up
Every vestige of knowledge she has for me
Drops of her essence that have become the proud
Anishinabe woman she is
She is around me and a part of me
And I am enthralled by her voice.

Everywhere

You are in the earth...
I send my fingers through and into
The deep dark soil
I take you in, breathe in the smell of life
Of rebirth and new beginnings

You are in the trees...
The long hands, fingers
Trailing against my skin
I raise my hands to greet them
Be embraced by them
Held by them in this world
Of complete silence
Except for the murmur
Of the leaves whispering,
I love you, I love you~

You are of the water...
It's waves lapping
Surrounding my legs
Wrapping around my body
Enclosing me completely
I lean back with no fear
Knowing I will be protected
Engulfed in your rhythm

You are of the wind...
Caressing my hair
Whispering words only

I can understand
Only I can interpret
Words meant just for me
Southern breezes traveling many miles
To meet me, greet me
As I breathe you in

You are in everything I touch
Everything I see, hear, feel and understand
Without the need of words.
You are everywhere.
Knowing this, I am never without you.

Fast

I'm preparing for a journey
Preparing for a fast
That my body and spirit are calling for
The spirits are telling me it is time
So I'm making the preparations
I'm talking with the healer
I know this sacrifice will not be just for me
But for all those that cannot do it themselves
The ones that need it more than I
Questions will be answered
More challenges will be put ahead
So I hold true to the sage
Hold tight to the sweetgrass and tobacco
When I see the eagles
I know Father is watching over me
As always, I am never alone
Gitche Manitou has blessed this place
Where I have grown into a woman
From the land I touch
To the water I drink
I am thankful my parents
Chose this place to settle
Their footsteps have been here for generations

Father's Hands

I will sing your song the rest of my days
Drumbeats, slow and steady
Like the heartbeat of my Mother
As I slept in her womb
Her voice intermingling with yours
Until they became one for me
In that one, I knew love and security
Strong hands held me, cradled me
Hands that had worked the woods
Hunted deer to feed his family
Worked in the assembly plant
These same hands promised to
Protect me with their touch
They never broke that promise
Every day I wake part of me knows
Admits, you are not here
Yet part of me feels you behind me
Walking in my footsteps
Whispering encouragement and hope
If I would stop….and listen

Ghost Dance

Like the Indians of old
Praying to the spirits during the Ghost Dance
He wore his courage like a Ghost Shirt, but
I knew he wouldn't be saved from the bullets this time
He fought for every new breath
For every new experience
Knowing it may be the last
He swallowed fear and the days before his death
Shook off fear like crystal snowflakes
He bound us to him with curled branches
Veins of blood and bones
His tracks left bear paw prints in the
Sand near Lake Superior that faded
As the tide claimed them once again
To be renewed when the tobacco was offered
As prayer is given, self sacrifice achieved

His conflicted spirit left so many times
But I knew I could never ask him to stay
I could never ask him to live bound in pain

I let him go.

We clothed him in his ribbon shirt
Sang the traveling songs for him and
When leaving the cemetery, I did as I was told
I did not look back, but waited
Until the eagles came for him.

Gimiwuna-gokwe

The window through your eyes is cloudy,
but I'll stay until the storm clears.
You are always in my prayers,
you are always in the tobacco I offer.
We are connected in ways no one understands,
we share the same sense of humor,
same style, taste, love of life and the mystery of it all,
ways in which we cannot explain,
spoken and unspoken,
but I welcome all that it brings.
I may not know what tomorrow will send,
but I will sit under your window and wait,
until you let me in.
You have been chosen special by the spirits,
they have plans for you,
always have directions for you,
always speak to you,
never fear their voices, strong one,
close your eyes and release.
Smudge and pray for the strength,
It will be there for you,
the Thunderbirds have chosen you,
you have a special power,
protect this power and nourish it to teach others.
Guide the younger ones....

Her Bone, Her Marrow

I come from my Mother's blood,
her bone, her marrow.

Born of the blood, the marrow
the center of which we all are
to unravel and slowly begin,
that journey to become my own Being.

To walk beside her,
hold her hand and match her footsteps,
to see my own eyes reflected in liquid pools
of black moons.

I sometimes follow behind,
walking in her footsteps,
as I walked in my Grandmothers' footsteps
and my ancestors before them.

My connection to that blood
is born of intense longing
to continue that bond,
of Grandmother/Mother/Daughter,
to know where I have begun,
to know of the blood I am born from,
to never forget it.

I come from my Mother's blood,
her bone, her marrow.

KBIC

I was born and raised on the Keweenaw Bay Indian reservation.
Here there is alcoholism, drug use and abuse of all kinds,
here there is also hope, love, kindness and strength,
most of all, perseverance and survival.
The elders tell us to hold on to our tribal tradition,
those traditions will bring us to a higher place.
Powwows, feasts and teachings bring us together,
unfortunately, so do wakes and funerals,
but love between family and friends is always there.
This love sustains us, binds us together.
There is a sense of urgency to our togetherness,
we are losing our elders, our oral traditions,
day by day, they are walking on to a better place.
We are left behind to piece together memories & photographs
from the whisper of the elders' voices,
tribal members are slowly learning our language.
Hope and dedication become strong forces in our fight.
This has become a fight to save our tribe,
we need to stay together,
stop the fighting among members,
create a plan to band together,
save this tribe for the younger ones.
Our lives are a circle, we are coming to the beginning once again,
such as our ancestors, we are battling to protect what is ours,
yet the enemy has already invaded our lands.
This time, it is not the white man,
instead it is alcohol, drugs, abuse and poverty,
it is the loss of language and culture,
it is the loss of life and history,

there is a call going out for our
Ogitchdaa and ogitchdaakwe to defend
we need to run for our stronghold.
Fight tooth and nail for what we have left,
take back what is ours.
Those members losing the substance fight,
we need to fight to save those warriors.
Use that love, strength and togetherness,
use our gentleness, our kindness,
everything that encompasses what we are,
to battles our enemies.
May our forces be many....

Lac Vieux Desert

This road fills my dreams
Mother says it is nine miles long,
full of twists and turns,
I can close my eyes and remember every curve.
Grandfather Frank Brunk Sr. walked this road every day,
Father Al walked it with his siblings to get to school.
This road connects Watersmeet to the old village,
when I visit this place, I offer tobacco to the ancestors and
my relations who have passed on.
This sacred place where Father was born and raised,
where my relations are buried and now rest,
I dream of it when I miss Dad the most.
I wonder what the village was like when he was young,
this place is where the eagles dance and connect with the
Anishinabe,
this place is held close to our hearts.
Generations have connected,
through the dances of old and
the powwows now held there.
If you close your eyes and listen quietly,
you can hear the old songs mingle with the new,
the dancers of the new powwows,
share these ancient grounds with the old ones,
whose dances now inspire them today.
My Grandparents brought their children up in the old village,
the foundation of their home is all that is left.
I took a brick home, one of the last times I was there,
It has a place of honor on my bookcase.
When I see it as I rise for another day,

I am pulled back to Lac Vieux Desert,
to the eagles, the voices held on the wind,
the dreams of my Grandparents so long ago,
that our blood would continue on.
I think they would be proud to know,
We as a family, are still here.

Lac Vieux Desert Part II

When my Father was five he contracted smallpox.
He was living in the old village with my grandparents and his siblings,
he had already lost two older sisters to the disease,
a disease that crept like fog into the small intimate homes of Lac Vieux Desert.
Slowly and methodically, it was picking and choosing from each family.

Dad had yet to attend school, but had been a student of
my great-Grandparents' all his young life,
he learned our connection to the animal brothers & our spirit helpers,
at birth, he was gifted with the name Nii-gwan-ni-gabo (He Who Leads).
From the time he could speak & walk, my Father spent his whole life
earning that name.

Before he became sick, my Father would go with his Mother (My Grandma Gabo),
they would assist the sick families, when no one else would.
It was understood why no one would, out of fear of sickness.
But my Grandmother couldn't stand to see anyone sick or ill, and not assist.

She sent word to another tribe for help.
This is how the fortunate events fell into place for Dad to be saved,
when my Father began to come down hard with smallpox.
From what Grandmother told, he had already started walking down the trail,
he had already heard the traveling songs from the ancestors on the other side....
When the medicine woman pulled him back to us, to his future family,

to his grandchildren and great-grandchildren still celebrating birthdays
every day.

Nii papa lived a good, strong life before the cancer took him from us.
We spent many days with him, enjoyed his laughter, his stories, learned
his advice.
We will forever hear him telling us right and wrong, and know he is never
far from us,
We may never know the medicine woman's name, but I am thankful
every day for her,
I hope on some level she is aware of the monumental effect she had on a
5-yr-old's life.

Chii-miigwetch.

Lingering

I've learned the hallways and shortcuts of Marquette General,
five different ways to the cafeteria, I have memorized the
schedules of the Oncology nurses,
I know Papa lingers in pain, sleep or no sleep.
Long distance phone calls, cafeteria food, living on caffeine,
its amazing what a body can sustain, what a spirit can hold up against.
But I not speaking of myself, I am speaking of Papa.
My Papa is loved I see it in everyone's faces,
in the gestures, hugs and kisses given, in the offers of support,
cards and flowers.....
But yes, also in: his tobacco pouch, his dreamcatcher, his eagle feather,
his sage, his braid of sweetgrass.
In his dreams, the spirits are speaking, telling him to come home.
Lately, he's been answering them. He catches himself speaking in
the ancient
language of the spirits through his morphine induced sleep.
He doesn't remember his dreams, nor of asking me of the elder
waiting patiently for him.
The elder only he can see, he only remembers he has a lot to say.
My Father. We talk into the night, with words and without.
He tells me everything he can, as if watching time slip from his grasp.
My father speaks, watches and waits....for rest.

Lingering II

In the early morning hours my Father relives his life,
the cancer invades his brain, he grasps those last evasive
coherent thoughts, and I watch him play catch with someone unknown,
he hits a homerun into the summer sun I cannot feel or see.
He smiles and lifts a shotgun and tells me to be still,
"Do you see that big buck over there? I'm gonna get 'em."
I encourage him, I know he will. My Daddy never misses.
Now and then in his lucid moments he watches over me,
As I fuss over his blankets, and prepare his morphine shot,
"I was talking goofy again, wasn't I?"
I merely smile at him and meet his eyes, squeeze his hand to show
him no words need to be said, I won't tell his secret.
My Father relives his life, talks with nephews who have already
passed on,
his Mother's spirit is in the corner waiting for him and I wonder….
When he will join her, when he will hear that traveling song and
follow it home.

Maiingan (*For David*)

You were five and wanted to push yourself on the swing,
"Auntie Sally, I can do it by myself."
My nephew with the dark brown curls,
dark sparkling eyes, always a smile on your face,
eager for hugs….affection.
During your visits to Grandma's on Mission Road,
you were too busy to listen to her stories,
too busy climbing trees,
playing with neighborhood children,
Grandma waited patiently,
knowing that soon you would climb in her lap and listen.
You would run home before dark,
before you could hear her stories or listen to the language,
you were nine, then ten visiting your Grandparents',
a quiet boy, it would take at least an hour,
to pull you out of your shell.
You then became the happy, smiling boy,
We had always known.
Sometimes you would play with the neighborhood children,
but preferred to walk alone in the woods bordering
your Grandparents' house
you wouldn't ask questions about the family,
would only go to powwows if asked by Grandma,
still….she waited for you.
I'd ask you questions about school and friends,
receive one word answers,
your interests always, one step ahead.
You became fourteen, fifteen,
a taller version of the boy we once knew,

who would sit in Grandma's kitchen eating cookies.
You were quiet, only coming to visit when invited,
sometimes just for Christmas Eve.
Grandma was happy to see you any chance she could,
I would watch her sitting in her room,
looking at photos of you by the light of her lamp,
she hoped for the day you would ask the questions,
you pushed everyone away, we heard rumors,
stories of the trouble you were getting into,
Grandma put down tobacco for you,
prayed you would find your way back.
You knew everything, wouldn't listen to pleas,
from your Mother, and Grandparents,
aunties who cared about you,
you became leader of a gang,
instead of a member of your tribe,
closed off your family,
closed yourself to traditions.
Traditions that could have,
helped you find your way.
You would talk to me
occasionally on the street,
ask for money,
I'd hand it over if I had it,
even though I knew it would come
to no good.
I felt helpless to stop,
The circle of self-destruction.
Your status as gang leader
became your undoing, your decline,
one moment of rage,
foolishness that you were a man,
handling a problem as a man would.

Now prison is your home,
you have nothing but time,
time to think about the family.
Traditions that could have been your anchor,
you're beginning to realize these are important parts of your life.
You are evolving into the man Grandmother always knew you
could be.
You're beginning to ask the questions.
Grandma is patient and still waiting for you.
Ask her the questions,
….she'll tell you the answers.

….Maiingan, you have become the man Nokomis always knew
you would become.
You respect your traditions, and have made a nice home. You
have two wonderful boys, Grandma is so very proud. Grandpa is
also proud, in the spirit world where we will someday meet him.
Keep them in in your heart your Grandparents will keep you
strong. Always honor your family.

Mama II

I watch my Mother when she doesn't notice me,
through the blue curtain that stands as her door,
I see the tiredness in her shoulders,
the pain pulsing through her back,
her eyes squinting to read the pages of her tiny paperback Testament.
In my thoughts I wish I could freeze this moment and
keep it in my pocket,
pray that she never relive it,
that this pain that visits her every night would disappear.
But it never does.
I come home from a long day of classes,
Monotonous trips through campus,
Hungry and frustrated with the constant war of words,
Sparring with my classmates,
Relieved once again to see my Mother's face.
I see her tiredness,
it saps her strength and pulls at her spirit,
but she doesn't relent and
I am amazed every day by her strength.
She has made hundreds of beds, thousands of loads of laundry,
stacks upon stacks of dishes.
She has kept a family of ten moving,
constantly moving through the ever evolving whirl of life.

She is the axis in which we revolve upon.

Each day that I see her face I am renewed
by her sense of spirit, of life.
Just to look at her and receive a smile,

I feel as if I can handle anything.
I can survive this chaos of school,
the migraines, sleepless nights,
Caffeine laden days and mental exhaustion,
are nothing compared to the power I am gifted
with by being her daughter.

Her blood flows through my veins.

Some shy away from comparisons with their mothers,
to be told they have their mother's
expressions, laugh, personality, her smile or her eyes.
I revel in the compliment.
She is everything I would ever hope to be,
everything I am thankful for.
Chii-megwetch nii momma.

Mama III

You cradle the most vulnerable part of me.
You have never looked away, turned your face
even when the trail has become treacherous,
when the rocky road has made my feet bleed,
you took care of me.

There are storms that have taken, drained my spirit,
you have picked me up and carried me.
I've wished for death, you chased it from my door,
you took care of me.

Last night, a thunderstorm arrived,
wind, rain, thunder & lightning,
it reminded me of what we have been through.
Together we have withstood worse without
the use of an umbrella, or my rubber boots.
You still take care of me.

Thank you for cradling me in sleep,
for waking me out of nightmares,
for being there in the darkest part of the night,
the time when everything is asleep.
When silence rules the night.

So I hoist this banner to you,
a flag I'll wave all my days.
I want to live in your house forever,
to explore its many rooms,
to look out its windows,

to know I am always welcome.
You still take care of me.

Mama IV

I'd like to think that I remember the very first time
I ever heard my Mother's voice,
I do know…it has always been there.
Whether I had hurt myself,
(Which happened a lot as a kid),
was sick or had a nightmare,
she was there.
Arms wrapped tightly around me,
soothing words to calm me ,
she is my constant.
She was there for all the big moments in my life
and continues to be.
She gives me strength,
when I feel too weak to stand,
she makes me laugh,
when I feel like crying,
She holds me,
times I need her to.
She is my best friend
I can tell her anything,
She loves unconditionally,
with her whole heart.
It's where I have learned
this most precious gift.
For her, I thank the Creator
every day of my life.

Cousin Mike

His posture is rigid and his profile is cut against the sun,
the backdrop is Lac Vieux Desert, the old village, "where eagles
dance."
I watch him every summer, his footsteps match the beat of the drum,
as all the flag bearers enter the the sacred circle
as he enters...
I look for him to enter, every time, every year, same spot.
The same emotions rise up, I feel great pride for all my relations dancing,
but I get a lump in my throat when I see my cousin Mike holding the flag,
as the flag is unwavering, as is cousin Mike, our constant.

Growing up, he is all we knew,
we ran to his arms for guidance when needed.
It was as natural there, as any older sibling,
His voice, his laugh, I have always known...
He is an amazing storyteller, weaves words like a blanket,
Now and then, he would tell stories when I was a child (still does, in fact).

When Mom talks of you, it is always with a smile on her face,
with love in her eyes, and deep respect,
this, we have learned from her, too.
But, respect is always earned by one who is a true warrior,
an ogitchiidaa of our tribe.
That is something you have earned with your actions and beliefs.

Because of our Grandparents, my parents, and cousins such as
you, Mike,
I, am proud of who I am,
I feel strong enough to write about our family & heritage,

I've learned who I was, and gave love because of it.

I say chii-megwetch to all my relations,
to my dear cousin, Mike who has given of himself,
to the Army & Tribal Police, and has made a beautiful family.
You & Joyce are such examples are what true family is, and does.

Lac Vieux Desert holds many memories for me.
But, I will always see your posture cutting against the sun...

I watched you tonight cousin,
Perfectly strong, yet filled with uncertainty
I knew I could not help you through this
Except with my presence and hugs, saying I love you
I have been in your chair and felt that tug, the silent scream
You know, he is so proud of this family
Sticking together, holding each other up
That's love.
That is what he taught all of us.

My Sister

When she is in deepest slumber
I feel the security of her presence
Knowing she is in the same house
Knowing the same blood flows through my veins
Makes me proud

She works as hard as our Father did
Sleep pulls her into it unrelentingly
Because she is a whirl of constant motion
Walking, doing chores, mowing the lawn

She has taken on responsibility asked of her and
Has responded as an Anishinabe woman does
She is a woman of her people and her tribe
They admire and look up to her

She is a woman of reverence
Who offers her tobacco and prayers
At sunrise and sunset
Communing with Gitche Manitou and the sun
That greets her every day

Because of her courage of meeting every day
Challenging every obstacle that comes the family's way
She has the love of her family behind her
I hope she always knows the pride we have for her
We would do anything for her
Because of the sacrifices she has made for us

Megwetch, my sister.

Nagwaan-nini-gabo

There are nights I still hear your voice break the silence in my room
The gruff, yet gentle manner of speaking you always had with
your family
We knew hearing that voice, everything would be alright
All of sudden, you call out my name and I am brought back to
your final months

Your endless pain, endured with a smile and a squeeze of the hand
Long nights spent talking of everything; pouring out your life as
quick as possible
My Grandmother's spirit calmly standing in the corner, waiting for
you to join her
I watched your conflicted spirit leave us so many times Daddy,
yet you held on
I knew you needed to hear the words…

Yet, here I sit fourteen years later and some days it is so very raw
& difficult without you
Some days I cannot stand, nor think beyond the fact of your
absence
Time does not heal all wounds, yet I can deal with the pain until I
see you again
I will be the kid you were once proud of

All of your children have moments of weakness, yet the Native
blood coursing
Through us says: Get up, there is work to be done. Hurt or not,
we move.
Our Mother misses you most, Daddy. Every day without you, we

do our best
To simply show she is loved & the most cherished person we have.

In the silence of 2am, Mama and I speak. She tells me of the
time, when she will
Walk the path and Papa and the ancestors will be waiting for her.
I don't cry, or get angry. I know this is inevitable. But it will be a
knife in my heart that nothing will ever change, no matter how
much time elapses.

But I listen, because I am the child who agrees it will be joyful
when she sees you, Papa.

Native Women

My dreams are of a journey
I am told I need to make
So I will spend the next year
Preparing for this task asked of me
Nothing about it will be easy
Yet I will never hesitate
Because it does my heart proud
As an Anishinabe woman
This is what I must do.

That is our tasks as Native women
Be proud and keep to family
Never forget to teach
Never forget the ancestors
I see this all the time
In my fellow sisters
It does my heart good
To see:

A woman with her child
A sister dancing in the arena
A woman offering tobacco
Women working in the health field
Fellow sisters fighting for Mother Earth's resources
Teenagers guiding the babies and children
The younger ones just learning to dance
Learning to weave words, beadwork & regalia
Learning to paint, sculpt and show others:

We are more than just painted faces.

Papa II

You have passed another birthday
And I quietly give thanks that I am
Here to share it with you.
My hope in this life is that you always know
I never wanted for anything in this world.
I was given all the love, affection and caring
A child could ever hope for.
In your presence I have felt security and unconditional love.
Its into your open arms that I have always run.
So today I praise you and all you have accomplished in this life.
Your love of athletics, your sense of humor
Your endless patience, your work ethic
And your strength in mind and spirit
Have all been passed on through your children
And your children's children.
I watch my brothers and sisters, nephews & nieces
And see the mannerisms, the laugh, smile or shining eyes
That have carried through generations.
Your presence is always here Papa.
Please know on this day how truly loved and honored you are.
You brought up children, grandchildren, and great-grandchildren
To love and care for their family.
Because of you, each one of them is strong.
There is no better lesson you could have taught us.
To me you will always be Superman,
You will always be my safe haven,
You will always hit the best homerun
And you will always be the most handsome.

Reawakening Of Spirit

My sleep has consumed me
It is this reawakening of my broken spirit
That has exhausted me
The strong healing auras and vibrations
That emanate from my fellow sisters
Who share my hotel room
Who share this reawakening in their own souls
We are growing and healing
Together and separately
Healing can be painful, yet necessary
Dreams swirl, whispering words in my slumber
I am not remembering my dreams
For two days, sleep has pulled me into its depths
Rest hasn't claimed me in over a year
Not since before my Father's passing
As we leave Minnesota and I look over its plains
I know it has revived me, given me back my spirit
Along with my sisters, who were there for me
I feel I can pick up my journal
I can look at the white expanse of paper and have courage
Passing through Nopeming, Dianna says,
"We are not returning the same women who began this journey."
I know she speaks the truth.

Remembering

What I remember from that summer of miserable heat,
were the flowers that bloomed regardless of the temp,
I remember surviving the June heat that nearly grabbed you
when you went outside, leaving you apprehensive in its wake.
I remember never waking in the same place twice and not
sleeping in my own bed for two straight months.
I came to realize one can get by on a couple hours of sleep,
one can semi-function because that is what is needed.
I remember my sister Brenda's yard filled with brightly
colored tents because we simply couldn't fit the whole
family in the house, I remember deliveries of groceries,
with a hug and no words because none was needed.
I remember Mom never leaving Dad's side no matter how
exhausted she was, only leaving when we put her to bed.
I remember our nephew Creighton sleeping in the chair next
to Dad talking sports until the late hours of the night because
that helped Dad keep his mind off of his pain.
I remember our cousins from Lac du Flambeau bringing the
drum to sing for Dad through the night, preparing him,
calming him for a journey that none of us could take with him.
What I remember, what I learned, what I realized is when Dad
left us he was surrounded by love, simply pure love.
We couldn't have sent him out in any better way than we did.

Still She Rises

The anniversary of my sister's death is upon us
Bringing up old memories
Sharp, agonizing ones and good laughter, rich memories
Both ending in tears

In the end we were gifted with my sister for 52 years
Before she walked on, leaving an imprint
That will never be erased or filled

Her smile so big & beautiful that her eyes would close,
Reminded me of our Dad
But her laugh…to hear her laughter in your day
Made everything feel right

Today I sit, watching the rain and listening to Mom sleeping
Her quiet even breathing
She is the strongest Anishinabekwe that I've ever known
I have known many

She survived much pain, physically & mentally
Pain that would felled many
Still she persists at 79
Losing our Father brought her to her knees
But losing her daughter took her to the ground.

Yet she rises.
Following her example, I rise.
Following her example, we all rise.

The Sacred

Have you ever seen the sunrise as it peeks over the eastern
doorway?
Stood on edge of Superior and offered your semaa for this day?
I know you have felt the peace that comes with walking at
Canyon Falls
All these places, my girl: Porcupine Mts, Tahquamenon Falls,
Kitchi-Iti-Kipii
We brought you to these places,

We brought all of our children to these places, to show them what
is right
To show them what is strong and beautiful in this world
This is what we, as Ojibwa have counted on for generations.
Earth, sky, plants, animals are cohesive & connected to us

We've wanted to show you where to find your peace,
To guide you to a place where you can lay down your prayers
To a place where you can commune with the Creator
Sacred places to not only the Anishinabe, but to all

For generations, your blood has walked these trails and paths
Gently, and quietly lived their existence, teaching the ways to the new
It is how it's done, it is how we survive and thrive
Elders hand down the knowledge, hand to hand, family ties are strong

Never forget the strong ties we have taught you, we have shown you
This is the sacred.

The Shack

In my dreams, I have visions of the shack that borne my family,
the trails through the woods that connected my parents to other members,
cousins, siblings running free in the woods, living off the land,
the creek that ran behind my Grandparents shack sustained them.
From a young age one learned how to hunt, fish and trap ,
my Grandfather Frank was a woodsman, as he taught my father to be.

My family never had much, but they always had love.
The young were taught by the old that you work hard every day,
that you appreciate what you have and always give thanks.

When they danced at gatherings it was in regular dress, not in regalia,
people knew what you were there for, no need for "extra dress,"
everyone was there to be healed, to celebrate and give thanksgiving.
Nii Mama says back then, people came from many miles to see each other,
simply to talk and share stories and wisdom; as it should be.
Life was good until the children were taken away to: Harbor Springs,
one by one…

After that, life changed. The children changed.
One by one, their spirits were slowly sucked from them.,
hollow shells, with empty eyes.

My brother suffered sexual abuse at the hands of the priests,
he drinks alcohol hoping to numb the shame and sickness he feels.
I see how it still takes pieces of him, year by year,

I pray all the time that he will one day, stand up and walk away
from the shame.

My sister suffered physical and emotional abuse from the nuns,
Constantly beat by them, told that she was a dirty, stupid, lazy child,
shamed into digging a graveyard with her bare hands,
small brown fingers meant to grasp swings not dig holes with
other children,
working underneath burning Midwestern sun, missing home....

All these children were scarred, scared and maimed.

My parents felt guilt for many years for letting their children go.
They carried guilt and shame that never should have belonged to them.
The boarding school gene has spanned generations,
Since the 1800's when they took the first child, until the last one in
the 1970's.

I pray every day for old ghosts and empty spirits.
I leave tobacco for my Father at his spirit house and ask for his help,
I smudge my Mother and thank Gitche Manitou that she is still
here with me,
most of all I ask for forgiveness, and humility. Every day I take a
deep breath, and start anew.

The Village—*For Stevie*

In my dreams I walk the trails and hills where our ancestors
walked, lived & died
I sit at the old village, the sacred ground where my relations' bones rest
I stand among their spirit houses; feel the power emanating,
passing through my bones,   pulsing like a heartbeat. Like a
heartbeat. Beat.

I feel it pulsing in my temples, through my heart, instilling my body
with strength.
Strength I feel from past experiences with them, their love, their
blood flowing;
        flowing like a river. Never- ending. This family bond will
never die.
This simple filament separating our worlds is but a simple step.
        That step on the path home to our relations. Someday.

But we must do our work here first. Lay the groundwork for the
next generation.
It is as it was, for the last generations. To teach, to love, to leave
when they feel we
        are ready. When we feel weakest, is when we earn our
highest warrior marks.
Our relations know when we are ready for bigger tasks; even
when we do not.
Never, ever count yourself short. You have cousins, uncles,
aunties, Grandparents and a loving Mother and Father standing
beside, and all around you. Always.
        They are your shield. They are your armor, so lean on them.
        Call on them. Cry out to them in anguish, in pain, or to share
happiness.

Our loved ones never truly leave us, it is merely another state of being.

Be strong, walk with confidence. Our ancestors are everywhere.
      They are where you are. Protecting. Providing. Smiling.
They are happy, and they want us to be happy. We'll feast when
we see each other again.
Until that day, let's teach what we have learned. Let's keep on learning.
I promised my Grandmothers' to keep learning, until I close
      my eyes for the final time, and take steps on the path home.

I know you. I know your heart. I have seen it in its darkest
moments. Yet even then it
      shined liked a beacon. You are a ray of light for so many.
Never forget your roots. Never forget your blood, and the soil that it
      comes from. This deep wild forest wilderness that is only
built for
      a certain kind of person. Few people can survive here. Only
the strong.

Your true friends, and the ones that love you, see the real you.
      In your eyes, they see the strength carried inside you. Not
just yours,
      but the beating of ten, a hundred, a thousand hearts inside you.
      The knowledge, history and survival instinct of a thousand years.
When you feel weak, feel your heart. Feel the beat of a thousand drums.
Feel the beat of a thousand years. Never stop listening. Never
stop fighting.

Until Home

When I was away at college
That was my first time living away from my family
At eighteen, I thought I craved freedom & independence

I come from warm loving parents,
I'm one of eight children
An aunt of (now almost sixty children) and
Our family boasts over 300 cousins
I come from clear night skies, often filled with northern lights
Blue grey water, moody & temperamental

College was a hustle & bustle of friends, class & caffeine
Filled with the sounds and pains that the city makes
But at night when I asked for sleep,
All that answered were traffic and sirens

There was no laughter at the kitchen table
Which was the main headquarters of our home
No voices that were the constant of my childhood, my upbringing
….my constant
No one teasing another with a joke or old story
Ah, the stories. How they fed me, and still do.

But at school I was starving.
Craving my family.
Calls home to Mom during Sunday dinner
Meant the phone was passed from hand to hand
Each with their own story, or joke about the week

Sometimes a random cousin dropped by
With drops of wisdom or encouragement
None of them aware of the silent tears rolling down my face
As I soaked up each voice.
Because I felt the sun in every single one.

With them, through them,
I lived to fight another week.
Until home.
Home

Voices That Carry Weight

Kaylee & I heard the distant drums calling,
The voices filling the silence of the night
Dark shadows coming around more,
Perhaps to warn us of coming pain?
I knew it meant something
But I never thought when I woke that day
That we would be losing you

Later that morning, as we were talking
We discussed how many of us had an awful night,
Trying to sleep the night before
Creighton woke at around three, and
Nancy woke around then too.

Mom couldn't sleep at all that night, she was restless
Kaylee heard whistling that night, and thought it was in the house
I was up around three, (couldn't sleep) and heard someone clearly
Call my name….
It was the way Dad used to call me through the monitor, when he
Needed me at night, except, it was a female voice.
I assumed it was Brenda's, since her bedroom was right down
from mine
I open my door and yelled, "Sister?" (Still sleepy) —to darkness
and silence.

No one there.

I wasn't really surprised by that, because Kaylee & I are gifted
with the ability to see and hear the spirits. Now and then, they
show up in the middle of the night.

See, that is their time.

Sharon, the moment, receiving the phone call, hearing Mother's
scream
I thought our hearts would literally break without you here with us
Every day is a fight, but we do it for you; Mama is being so strong.
When I wish for another moment with you, I remember how
happy you are
You are with our ancestors, whole & laughing—yes, and I hope
dancing
We laughed one day, about you getting a Harley. I hope you are
riding all over with Ricky, while you watch Dad's softball games,
maybe even watching a boxing match of Uncle Billy's. Now that,
would be something beautiful. Poetry in motion, I'm told.

So, I promise as your sister I will wish you beautiful moments,
happy times w/
Our ancestors & friends that have passed on. I will try not to cry
so much.

Warrior Women

I have been beaten for being Native,
for the warrior woman inside of me
for the Anishinabekwe who fights for her family
who fights for her tribe and clan.
Simple hatred does not understand,
it will not defeat me, will not faze me.
except for the scars I carry,
I carry those with pride because I survived you.
I keep the faith of my Grandmothers and Grandfathers,
their voices with me always.
In the wind that rushes over me
as I walk next to Lake Superior,
as I look over the red cliffs,
As I stand in the forest of white birch,
voices echo and footsteps are heard
of elders long past.
I will follow the footsteps
let them carry me home.
These voices have taught me so much,
I give thanks every day,
my thoughts are always with them,
feasts are offered,
the spirits are taken care of and honored.
because I survive, I become stronger,
because I offer tobacco I am stronger,
acknowledging the spirits makes me stronger.
Warriors lead by example.
Are you a warrior?

What My Father Was

My Father wasn't just a husband-married for over 47 years
Wasn't just a Father-to eight children
Or an uncle-to many nephews and nieces
He was also a coach to many softball and baseball teams
He was an umpire to many softball games, a referee for many
basketball games
My Mother still has his whistle, and pulls it out every now and then
He was also a serious man, I seen Dad cry only once, at his
Mother's funeral
I held his hand I watched his tears flow, doing the only thing I
knew to do, and squeezed his hand
But yes, he could be a funny man also he did crazy dances for my
Mother when no one else was looking,
He did those dances just to see her smile and laugh
He could tell the craziest stories, one was amazed by the fact that
they were true
He was very easy going and could get along with anyone
He could start a conversation with any man, woman or even a child
With each person falling in love with him just a little
Enough to stay loyal to my Dad and remember him whenever
they saw him again
I loved driving into town with him watching him wave to everyone
Some of the people he knew very well, some people he didn't
know at all
He was involved in so many different sports, that's how he met an
unbelievable amount of people
When he passed away, I remember looking through the back
window of the car after the funeral

I watched the line of cars through my tears and I silently thanked all those people for remembering my Father, for thinking of him on that day and taking time out of their lives to say goodbye

Whenever I am in town, and run into someone who knew my Dad, They simply say, "That was a good man."

That makes me feel good, makes me smile and I am proud once again that he is my Father

I know somewhere he is watching his family, he sees it growing one grandchild at a time

He sees all of them, sees all of us and in each of us he sees the mannerisms of my Mother, of himself

In this, I know my Father knows a piece of himself, will always be here Always.

What Price

What is the price of love that a woman has to pay?
Is it the split lip, black eye, or blood that covers my sister's face?
Hit because her boyfriend's nap was disturbed
Is it the cracked ribs or concussion inflicted on my friend?
Her husband's jealousy rears its ugly head daily
Her tears and blood falling on the emergency room floor
I have wiped so many tears, from too many faces
Is it the price of love, that days later
My sister's boyfriend is back,
Sucks her back in with flowers and soothing words
He punishes her for calling the cops
Throws her down a flight a stairs
Sending her to the emergency room this time
This time
Is it the price of love when my friend
Seeks her own revenge after her husband
Begins to hit the children without regret
SNAP
Runs down her husband with his own car
As he leaves the bar at two am
Seeing and hearing nothing when her foot hits the gas
Feeling….only peace
She is but a victim in a war, a vet of many battles
She has the scars to prove it
But her victory, her freedom is not celebrated
She is caged like a prisoner of war
Because she spilled his life into the gutter

Wigwam

She lives in a wigwam deep in the woods
Surrounded by pine, birch, oak and the smell of cedar
Far from noise, traffic, people…far from me
She handles solitude well
Tortures me with her delicate balance
No need of company
A fierce independence
A world void of conversation and meaningless words
Choosing company at her leisure
This forest its carpet of moss and pine needles
A blanket of fallen leaves
Her friend, her companion
This forest surrounds her clear distinct gaze of coal
I have felt that intense gaze
I relive it without fear

When The Darkness Comes — *For Ronnie*

My brother's room is next to mine
He tosses and turns, has nightmares
Fights his demons in restless slumber
Sometimes I watch him sleep
I wish I could bring him peace
He stumbles on the walk, falls on the stairs
At closing time, I hear my brother come home
My brother talks to himself
He cries when he thinks the house is asleep
Inebriation is a numbness he strives for
When memories swim to the surface
When the darkness comes....
Memories of the sexual abuse
At the hands of the priests
The strong, sweaty hands yanking him
Roughly up out of bed, pulling at his pajamas
Whispering threats and promises of punishment
His shame swallowed with his rage
Emotional abuse at the hands of the nuns
Dirty, stupid, lazy
His family's way of living, his life worthless
Unless he grasps this foreign faith
Authority figures he must obey
Figures responsible for assimilating little heathens
Into a better world (their world)
I listen in my own bed
Choke back my own tears
My own anger
I was never there, cannot imagine his pain

Cannot fathom the depths it reaches
What dark corner he pushes it into
To hide his shame
Shame that shouldn't belong to him
My brother's room is next to mine
Sometimes I watch him sleep
I wish I could bring him peace.

And the continuing words:
by Bamewawagezhikaquay

Here in my native inland sea
From pain and sickness would I flee
And from its shores and island bright
Gather a store of sweet delight.
Lone island of the saltless sea!
How wide, how sweet, how fresh and free
How all transporting—is the view
Of rocks and skies and waters blue
And all unites in sweetest strains
To tell, here nature only reigns.
Ah, nature! here forever sway
Far from the haunts of men away
For here, there are no sordid fears,
No crimes, no misery, no tears
No pride of wealth; the heart to fill,
No laws to treat my people ill.